Under a Future Sky

Under a Future Sky

poems

Brynn Saito

Red Hen Press | *Pasadena, CA*

Book design by Mark E. Cull.

Library of Congress Cataloging-in-Publication Data

Names: Saito, Brynn, 1981– author.
Title: Under a future sky: poems / by Brynn Saito.
Description: First Edition. | Pasadena, CA: Red Hen Press, [2023]
Identifiers: LCCN 2022055669 (print) | LCCN 2022055670 (ebook) | ISBN 9781636281070 (hardcover) | ISBN 9781636281421 (paperback) | ISBN 9781636281087 (ebook)
Classification: LCC PS3619.A3987 U64 2023 (print) | LCC PS3619.A3987 (ebook) | DDC 811/.6—dc23/20221125
LC record available at https://lccn.loc.gov/2022055669
LC ebook record available at https://lccn.loc.gov/2022055670

Publication of this book has been made possible in part through the generous financial support of Denise Frost.

The National Endowment for the Arts, the Los Angeles County Arts Commission, the Ahmanson Foundation, the Dwight Stuart Youth Fund, the Max Factor Family Foundation, the Pasadena Tournament of Roses Foundation, the Pasadena Arts & Culture Commission and the City of Pasadena Cultural Affairs Division, the City of Los Angeles Department of Cultural Affairs, the Audrey & Sydney Irmas Charitable Foundation, the Meta & George Rosenberg Foundation, the Albert and Elaine Borchard Foundation, the Adams Family Foundation, Amazon Literary Partnership, the Sam Francis Foundation, and the Mara W. Breech Foundation partially support Red Hen Press.

   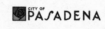 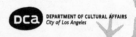

 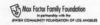

First Edition
Published by Red Hen Press
www.redhen.org

Printed in Canada

ACKNOWLEDGMENTS

Grateful acknowledgment is made to the publications in which versions of these poems first appeared:

American Poetry Review: "Given Name"; *The Atticus Review*: "Ordinary Animal"; *Discover Nikkei*: "Dear Reader"; *Gulf Coast* "Online Exclusives": "Days I Can't Feel You"; *Leaning Toward Light: Poems for Gardens & the Hands That Tend Them*: "Dear Damselfly"; *Nisei Radicals: The Feminist Poetics and Transformative Ministry of Mitsuye Yamada and Michael Yasutake* by Diane C. Fujino: "Lines for a Future Child"; *Poetry Northwest*: "Self Disguised as Stones"; *Poets.org's* Poem-a-Day: "How to Prepare the Mind for Lightning"; *Santa Monica Review*: "Letter to My Father"; *Sijo: An International Journal of Poetry and Song*: "Three Sijo"; *Tupelo Quarterly*: "Last Lines (I)" and "Last Lines (II)"; *The World I Leave You: Asian American Poets on Faith & Spirit*: "Turn to Ash"; *The Volta*: "Thirteen Ways of Looking at a Teacher Resource"; *Waxwing Literary Journal*: "Theses on the Philosophy of History" and "February 19, 1942".

This book was created with support from an Artists Initiative grant from Densho, the Santa Fe Art Institute's Truth and Reconciliation residency program, the Hedgebrook Writers-in-Residence program, the Napa Valley Writers Conference, and the College of Arts and Humanities at California State University, Fresno. Special thanks goes to Traci Brimhall, Brandon Shimoda, Corrinne Clegg Hales, Lee Herrick, Brian Komei Dempster, Jaime Rodríguez-Matos, Venita Blackburn, and Valarie Kaur for their careful review and feedback of early drafts of the manuscript. Many thanks to the entire team at Red Hen Press for their literary labor and love.

Thank you to my fellow Central Valley writers and poets; my colleagues in the English and Creative Writing program at Fresno State; Jason Bayani, for getting me writing again; and my Yonsei Memory Project sisters, Nikiko Masumoto and Patricia Wakida. It's good to be home, memory-keeping and community-building alongside you. To all of my students over the years: your work and our conversations continue to expand my understanding of poetry's possibilities. Thank you.

To family and friends whose voices are featured here: you took a leap with me and for that I'm deeply grateful. To my husband, Dave Lehl, title-finder: thank you for your strength and boundless love, especially through the dark times.

Lastly, gratitude to my elders, my ancestors, and our ancestors of the future.

For Gregg Saito
and Janelle Oh Saito

CONTENTS

I

II

III

Under a Future Sky

What or how did you feel when you visited Poston and Gila River?
What or how did you feel when you stood there, surrounded by what
must feel like both the emanations of the past and the sharp, biting
pains of the present? What does your father have to say about all this?
—Brandon Shimoda, personal correspondence

I am memory alive.
—Joy Harjo, lecture, Jack Kerouac School of Disembodied
Poetics

DEAR READER

Do you believe in the wide open
       privacy of the desert, do you believe
              in the prophecy of stones? My desire

for you is eternal and makes you eternal.
       My desire's the shape of three columbines
              blooming in a cracked riverbed.

Do you believe in the distant silent
       company of the women in your family,
              the continuity of the clandestine?

Do you memorialize wire, do you
       ritualize joy? I want to fall nightly
              to the sitting place where ghosts visit,

draw a bath for the goddess of all things
       that flow: Water, words, time. Speech, sound,
              knowledge. Were you afraid

of what you might say to yourself in the face
       of the page's stillness, under the hailstorms
              of an arid high desert? I was afraid.

So lonely at the writing desk, I imagined you
       drinking midnight tea, or turning your face
              to the shameless marigolds, or rising

with your daughter's cry in the blue light
of dawn. Do you imagine me?
    None of the fires have forgotten you

don't tell me otherwise. Forgive the rotting daikon
the gobo overgrowing the old yard.
    I've made a ceremony of ghosts.

I

LETTER TO MY FATHER

What's ironic, Brynn—my parents wanted to forget this
place—but I want to remember it.
—Gregg Saito

There's a new way I see the garden now

the one you've been tending for decades on Garden Avenue

(of all names)—the street of our family home.

In haiku written by camp prisoners,

days and seasons are tracked by the falling leaves

of the moss rose, petal to earth. Poets in camp

numbered months and years by the memory

of their home gardens left behind on the West Coast:

flowering rhododendrons and peony buds they imagined

as vibrant, their stalks remaining firm. I think of us,

traveling that week in the summer of 2019, away from California,

along the train's course, through Arizona, and on to Poston

and Gila River. How far I brought you from your garden.

Did you think of the sagos, the summer tomatoes

and basil, the azaleas and red maples, the night-blooming

lantana, trees needing trimming, grass going brown—

all the work awaiting you? Did you imagine

the dog's chirping, the silent, white bucket, and Mom

dragging the hose across the lawn to wake the fountain?

Here in the Southwest, I find myself pining

for the Great Central Valley, as I did when I lived in New York

or that decade in the Bay, exhausted from cold bridges

and colder waters, longing with my entire body

for the landscapes of childhood's kingdom. Smog-dust and all.

I understand now I am nothing. I'm the daughter

of a living father, blessed to be returning to you

after our fire-and-ice travels through North American

landscapes spotted by our elders' lives, their prison

desert homes, and other jails and prisons—with

and without bars or barbed wire. You were not taken.

In the night and shirtless, you were not captured

or broken by the sentry's light, despite my nightmares.

You took your time in the summer garden, where Leigh

and I played as the light set, basil-ing our bodies

against mosquitoes, baking mud-sweets in California's

sugary dusk. Dad, your voice is wise now, beyond kindness.

I'll see you soon.

—*June 14, 2019. Santa Fe, NM.*

SHE ARRIVED

for Tamayo Teranishi

She arrived on a boat with a photograph
of her future husband who was not the man
who greeted her. Some of the women

with her on the boat went into
the fields, toiled down the days,
never slept soundly. Some of the women

rode into cities to serve other women
and men. She made her way to the Great
Central Valley—harvest of the nation, dusted

with sunlight, blood-struck fields—to labor beside him.
Of the children she bore, some survived her.
Others did not. All were swept up

and shuttled into horse stalls when the Great War
tolled itself across the nation, that bell-dawn
of violence. Later in the little wooden house

planted in the middle of the valley town
she in her nineties drank beer and hollered joy
at the TV screen. Her beaded eyes

and bun of black hair never faded to white.

Self Disguised as Stones

after Gila River

1.

Were I there   under eave and uncrushed

set in some   dust corner after desert snow—

Were I riparian spec   alkaline and present

aventurine redressed   mountain chip, moss rose—

What could I speak?

I might have soaked   secret after secret

seen spark birthing seed   birthing daughter and sons   their unwired love—

I might have drank joy   from the blameless

seen meeting of the gambler   and survivor of addicts

two laboring landless—

For years I was restless

amethyst disguised as ash rock   freckled, forgotten

noctilucent daikon—

I was afraid of my face

2.

She walks through constructed silence

arousing memory.

She follows the long-limbed

beetle over quantum mountains

arresting memory.

Of Capricorn and Gemini

of nebula and violin:

one daughter of queens wandering creosote.

Of Milky Way and wonder throne

of swallow tail and milkweed:.

hearty grass and omen ants gather.

Birds trill electronic.

A cloudless sulphur catches light.

She lets me down slowly.

3.

I was there. I was restless—

my mind, a body

my body sweeping life's cells

in a single direction

over Earth's face—

sea freedom for centuries

a chemical fist

unfolding in the fescue.

Desire did this:

fertile dust and diatom seas

forest lung and red rock—

a roiling grace.

You die. I collapse in the hollow

before language:

knot in your father's throat

in Hiroshima

everlasting rock monument

writing on the crane's wing

folded by the dead one

under a future sky.

4.

I'm single stone with dual souls:

two, then three   handfuls of rock-shard under dim

immense heaven.

One conflict illuminates the other—

hexagonal suffering in sky time   over moonstone super enemies.

I'm talking   about the garden now

how it stared down the wolf-heart   won.

Roots hold on to each other   uncapsized

under August soil—   sheer history   traveling underground eros.

One cross holds the sea dogs at bay.   The other archives light.

Un-beast me.   Pack of dogs   take my palm.

Open me to the secret memory.

FEBRUARY 19, 1942

Moon across the sky in the purple morning
dry earth unfurling.

In another California
my grandmother is packing

everything she owns into one suitcase
two suitcases, the water still

in the clay pitcher—water unwasted
only what she can carry.

There is no moment in my life
in which this is not happening.

What is happiness? Two granddaughters
in a summer garden—

firstborn, second born—and grandmother
laughing. There is no moment

in which she is not alive
and rising, imbuing these hills,

this morning's sky with shadows.

Thirteen Ways of Looking at a Teacher Resource

What types of memories have you inherited?

Stories live in me like sharp lightning flashes across a southern desert.

How have they been passed down to you?

She said: *On the train*
they packed us like sardines
or *We drove our own cars to the camps*
or *I wore a button*
during the war saying
"*I am Korean*" *for protection.*
Then nothing.
Then great seas of silence
death-quiet and dark
that swallowed us.
Then cans in the backyard
crushed and recognizable.
Then light in a box
rain in a box. Azaleas.

What helps you remember them?

If you get your face quiet enough, what counts as your father's shadow
will speak through it.

How have they impacted your life?

Into the night and into the streets
of the universe I walk with my little
blue heart. I rise my hands
to the fractured light
like the girl I was, aching for safety
and rehearsing my freedom
in the garden under my father's
sky. I got close to whiteness
by fear-loving my uncle: him and mercy me
shooting guns in the foothills
while the great spirit cloistered itself
in the dying oaks of an earlier
century. Now the air turns.
The moonlight eats us happily
and we're happy for it.
Little hummingbird ghosts gather
in a field far from here plotting
their revenge. My uncle grows older
and closer to death near a trailer park
in the Central Valley. I grow a skin
beyond my skin, rage swelling me
beyond the perimeter of my known self.

Do you think they've changed over time?

Stories live in me like sauntering fireweed, misplaced cell clusters,
schools of stones.

Do any of these inherited memories relate to historical events?

I tell my students: There's no part of us that goes untouched by the
angel of history, wings pinned to the air by the storm of progress.

What memories of your own have you chosen to share with others?

The light sings itself awake.
I'm awake at the turn
of the twenty-first century
and alive to the turning.
Did I ask too large?
I'm afflicted with desire
and the girlhood wish
to lay my body down
in the blue summer grass
lit and unlit by the flicker
of the setting light.
Though shapes and faces
sail down the bloodlines
though ghosts grow their nails

into me, I remain a romantic.
For years, I turned the fire
inward, bleeding to prove
how much I wanted to be here
and break the skin and belong
in ways undreamt by them
to the administered world.

What are the differences between memory and history?

One gives birth to fire and one gives birth to stones.

Do you think history is fixed or objective?

No.

What is the relationship between the past and the present?

Yes.

How do we make meaning from the past?

Yes.

How do you make meaning from the past?

See the writer again at the gate of memory?
See the writer again—
See the writer again at the gate?
Gate the writer again at the memory—
See the past again at the meaning gate?
Past the making, gate the memory—
See the meaning?
She should drink.
She should drown it.

Do you think we have a responsibility to the memories we inherit?

"Even the dead," wrote Walter Benjamin, "will not be safe from the enemy if he wins."

Theses on the Philosophy of History

or *Listening to the Presidential Debate While Stuck in Traffic*

1.

Roads clog with people in vehicles crossing the Golden Gate
Give my rage back to me, I know how to hold it
Ghost fog grows and stretches itself through the bars and I'm ready for it
On my radio, the white general and the white general
yank each other into the deep end, good heavens
Don't teach me to hate my language tonight
Don't teach me how to hate my lips and their language tonight
Tongo says capitalism walks on water, I've seen my TV, I believe it
All of the redwoods in the world can't keep this country from wanting to die
The future has arrived and it's doubled over
and the best of us are ready for love though we're burning

2.

Roads clog with people in vehicles crossing the Golden Gate
My family is Eduardo and Mitsuo and Marilyn and Alma
and Samuel and Fumio and the twin who drank himself to death
and the auntie who drank herself to death
and the Issei and the Nisei and the Sansei with their rock faces and nightmares
Undisguise me, said the stone
Undisguise me, said the stone to the desert light
Undisguise me, said the stone to the river
Lay me down under harsh water flowing under midnight starlight
Take my face off of my face, said the stone, shake me open

3.

Roads clog with people in vehicles crossing the Golden Gate
The white general and the white general
teach me how to hate my language on the radio tonight
Which nightmare of a framework makes the human count
Which bodies count and which count against
Grandma met Grandpa in those camps
Let me give your rage back to you, said the poem
Stop trying so damn hard, said the poem
Everything that has ever happened to you and your family
keeps happening and the love keeps coming in with its surgery
Get good with yourself, said the poem, get gone

Prayer for a Trembling Body

after Atlanta, March 16, 2021

Queen of adrenaline: come to me with
your clear wings. Queen of the breathless
season of shelter: I'm swelling with
blossoms in the Great Central Valley,
I'm trying to have a child and raging for a
sign, I'm pressing my luck against Trump
flags flapping over black trucks sunrise
piercing the Sierras.

Daughter of un-barracked deserts and
trauma, queen of cerebrum and spinal
cord seas: *We survived* says my mother,
no grocery store murder, no white pow-
er virus. Tell me, why are we only made
visible by violence? We're aloe in the long
leaves of the childhood garden. We're un-
dammed free waters rivering grief.

Queen of the blood-brain barrier burn-
ing, daughter of scapegoat expressive
depression: it's night in the sweat-bed.
In one dream, all the swords with their
skull handles pierce the snow stag. In an-
other, I float happy and unclothed under
gnarled oak and lotus.

Dear radical ancestor: I'm eating their language. Help me set down my husband's gun, unstitch my eyes. Show me post-memory ghosts in the name of new justice. Bring me sister-mouth refuge in the moon-washed, dog-snarled irreversible night.

Self Disguised as Memory Hunter

after Poston and Gila River

1.

Concerning the spiritual in art
the mauve mountain
and the woman by the roadside
divining a life beneath the cut horizon—
Do we dare hunt memory?

Smoke hunts me.

I night-fly over strong grass and confessional mesquite—
a new moon's witch flight.
I try and the trying
disappears things: gambling games, border rivers
bullet flecks, gardens.

I stretch the bone of my mind's eye over the old settlement
from outfield to olive tree, from father's father
to father's mother
from fire silk to sentry

and something of a picture of love emerges.

2.

"Feel America
Live America
Love America
Then work"

What have I killed with my hands?

Sometimes even succulents die
and orchids easily
or sweetgrass
or chard.

I roam:
Fever ice, violent blossom.

I de-root and distance.
I desert and dance myself into open fields.
I delight in departure.

3.

Hot bones of North America, remember me.

Hunt down places pain craters: lateral dorsal and left shin
mother's neck, father's skin
late summer lump and the optic nerve
where light loosens.

Take these ankle chords, this womb-scar, hip fluid and nipple.
Take belly fire, cloud-palms,
violet eye, spine bloom—

Here there is no whaling.

No one is absent.
Creosote, re-member.

Hot bones, re-member me.

4.

What have I hunted?
What will I haunt?

I become dirt death and star bath—
art in another century.

I become singular and multi-life,
disordered creation, glowing oak canopy,

moon planet, grace portal,
Bermuda vortex, singing bowl.

I become story-silk and lost song,
single note middle C

ringing in the houses of my children's
children's children.

LOVE POEM FROM ANOTHER DIMENSION

If upon waiting you find it
hard to put down your lung
to rest a little and lean into
the sun setting beyond
the bleachers of youth, don't
worry. If grass turns blue
and bottles start to
reassemble themselves
don't think too much of math
or gravity. Ten times over
I've returned to you wholly
and freely glowing
with the kind of starlight
that takes eons to get here.
I walk to you always
from the other dimension
where we've met again
as goldfish, where we've
met again as cinquefoil
where, in the waters of sky
our mindless, bodiless
spirits swim in snow.
I believe in a goodness
that will not break
a goodness in your boy hands
a goodness in the letters
that made it to the desert
camp, a sweetness that memory

makes sweeter. If upon waiting
the decades spill out of you
and suddenly you're ninety
and the absent bleachers
and summer fields
of our candied youth
burn circles in your blood
don't worry. I lived.

Questions for the Tarot on My Fortieth

Do you wear midday's fire-smoke like a loose garment?
Is the new moon pregnant with night or sun-shy?
How ugly do I need to become to myself before I trust this marriage?
If my child-self could rename God would she fear volcanoes?
Will you bury my body in the apocalypse garden?
Will I learn to swim clockwise around a future child?
Is my spirit a keyhole or a lock in the earth's crust?
Am I alive in the union of dead ash and stream?
Am I alive in the milk-shaped container for love?
Am I alive in the dialogue between undead and undead
or un-antlered silence, misting through forest for the highway?

LETTER TO MY GRANDMOTHER

*I imagine us at Gila River, walking together to the half-circle
monument of stark white pillars at the top of the rocky hill that
overlooks the desert which once caged our grandparents. In this
vision of us together, I can let my heart-space soften.*
—Nikiko Masumoto

Grandmother, were you with me in the writing studio

surrounded by penciled facts and your son's face;

in the park with the low rock memorial;

in the walk through canyon trails and ghost reservoirs

cooing with cattails; in mountain baths

with white bodies and wet wood? Were you with me

in Arizona or the Eastern Sierras, when I stood beside

your son and his wife, my father and mother:

three in the cooler desert, correcting memory?

I recall your dying and the days that followed—

your body mourned and buried, then called back again

in seven days, then forty-nine, then one hundred, and one year on—

the smoking ash in the iron bowl, incense seducing air.

I remember running a stiff brush over your tender scalp,

your mouth pulled in a closed pain, your death wish,

uttered aloud from the hospice bed

in the spring living room and me, little, hearing it.

Grandmother, I've grown close to these high desert blooms—

the common yarrow and salvo, the rows of petunia;

I feel the place unfolding in my blood like a new story.

This evening, hailstorms praised the Sangre de Cristo

mountains, ridges alive in the pounding light.

Empathy is a smooth stone that cuts sometimes,

says my friend here. Freedom is pliers gripping

a rotten tooth. Democracy is the blood of Christ

turning into mountains. A portal closes. My time in the desert

is coming to an end. There's no way to imagine

your young life enduring the camps, except in dream-poems,

except through archive-shadow, except in the cards

upturned on the mystic's table in the middle of the wretched

summer basin, shot through with mesquite and buried laughter.

Grandmother Alma Teranishi Saito, you are missing.

I am missing you.

—June 19, 2019. Santa Fe, NM.

LAST LINES (I)

Mutant, you said and we understood.

Moonlight unlocks murder dreams, the angels sober.

In the mystic classroom, we clapped our hands at the seeds of sacred dignity sewn into the skin of Western philosophy.

Simple.

The cells marched.

Mother, you re-mother.

Bones bloomed and the bodies once inside your body got blessed by city light.

Toadflax, loosestrife, foxglove—

What silently praises the sun?

None of the fires remember my name, lie near to me now.

Gallop alongside your animal fear and the addict who loves you.

Tumble and scar, the mountain will teach you.

I'm a coin on the lake-face—

Windless, moonless, triple-threat ghost.

Who you've been can no longer carry you.

That's the miracle.

II

Ordinary Animal

1.

Given Name

No one tells me how to name it, I name it
    animal. I tell it *never come*. I watch it
        strengthen on the fever farm, take tendon

after tendon, lift its own spoon
    at the family table, taste. I watch it grow tall
        with the family's starch and salt

the sweat and the family's wide-awake
    eyes staring like light beams
        at the all-night ceiling, fear fuel.

No one tells me how to name it
    I name it *animal*. I name it clean-crushed
        beer can, cop-outfit calling, binge dawn.

I tell it *come here*, come willing to dance, say:
    take me by the eyes and explain
        yourself and your blood time

with this blood life—this river family
    that valley farm. I say, What took us down
        that day, river-worn, wordless?

What takes us down, animal? Explain you.

2.

Origin Story

Tiny islands
       rumbling countries

crested peninsulas—
       surrounded.

Two nations susceptible—
       tsunami violence

fertile fears—
       teething at one another's

necks, locking one another's
       hearts in colonial arms.

Outside the temple
       on the left side

of moonlight, upright
       impressive ears

stalking the river ridge.
       Shacks

in the outer city
     rice paper winds:

one mother
     drawing blood breath

out of the other son—
     second born, sacrificed—

the snarled face of you,
     patient, waiting.

Who was the first
     to take you, animal?

Who was the first
     to take you down?

3.

Animal Under Rafter Shadows, Watching

Farmhouse with her father
                    facing the barrel of *No*

            Shotgun shadow

                        You must
                        choose

                                    anyone else

        Pomegranate desire, pitchfork knowing—
Him

I hook my life to him

                        Dust temptations, liquor-hot omen, clock-face of death

        Father of my son
        My daughter
        My son

4.

Believe in a Power Greater than Sanity

But the animal   is an animal   and we are

Rage tooth and white eyes   seven claws   resting now

She looks like the little one
I wanted to tuck under me   wing under my wing
to watch her   I wanted fierce to fold her
as if I were mother
not sister   lover-protector
not sister   oak and mighty ginkgo root
not girl-growing
choking weeds in the blue ruin

The animal wants to   lay down its teeth   wants to
stop-gnaw   call me
wants to place its gray blood-brow
on my little lap   fall there

What was it   I wanted?
To sleep beside her
merge dreams   To walk together
in the water kingdom
two peacetime soldiers   resting

5.

Our Lives Restore Us to Our Lives

Every night not knowing
          what shape the animal
will take, whether the kittens

have eaten and where
          in the mind one's fear-body
resides. Returning home

to what fires in the heart
          what figures making drunken
shadows over kitchen grass.

Sometimes there's a shriek
          loose in the house—a darting
thing. Sometimes there's one hand

holding another in deliverance.
          To live with the animal, unseen
and everywhere, is to hunker.

To find in oneself a stillness
          the shape of an orchid
is nothing short of rebellion.

6.

We Were Powerless

No one ever told me, ghosts.
No one has ever

                     shaken me awake

sputtering tongue-truths
       ready to tell.

No one took me to the sago
                  safe place

shook my palms, looked me in the heart:

                  Hold still in the sober kingdom, no keys.

Nobody
       came for me, you didn't

know how to, you didn't
know how

to breathe underwater

you didn't understand we were breathing

                                   underwater

you did what was best of you—

you gave it. Nobody
                          told us how to do it.

And who told you?

No one.

7.

My Shortcomings Make a List

Tupperware and spoons tell me:
     get your own life.

So I go into the night
     away from the burning kitchen, I scale

the houses, walk across roofs,
     step into sky, stairs invisible.

Below me: the leaning cypress, the upright palm,
     two boys rushing the beach

in matching shirts—*hug it out,* they say.

What if our birth order
     were switched? As the younger

would I warp myself
     around her survival? Gulls skim the surf.

Someone handwrites
     into his journal and smokes.

I want to prove my love and prove
my worth. Rocks slip the sea

in their perfection. Mind and body
bob and wander with the foam below.

8.

Animal on Vacation

Animal come home to me   come praise.

These tooth days find me foraging without you   your body
on the farther island

licking wounds.

I miss your power.
Fear my own.

Love is a political gesture.
Mornings teach me who I am.

I crawl around the bathroom floor
tears make a cityscape   tile is a wedding.

I press my cheek against it.

9.

Fearless Persons Injure God

My love and I wonder what's in us—
    what rivers. Half-lit valley sky

sheets slight with wet. Us
    in the after-blood, before babies

get born, before rivers fold over
    their double life, before blood
does its helix dance with history.

    I'm guessing gun shapes
sago gardens. I'm guessing war time
    tin hearts, mother-worry.

What more can we measure
    make sense of with mad math, we don't
matter. We don't want to die either

    we don't want each other
to die. But the animal we know
    eats everything. The animal

on a blood run has a mind of her own.

10.

Her Sobriety is a Mountain in the August Dark

I had a vision:

Two queens, no war.

Private taste of pine and the light chorus.

Rock dawn and night worry—
        impetus of bark, the inner flare.

Animal, free you. Like daughterhood
goes away—
go away.

Do you trust the hawk's blooming circles?

It's time.

11.

Ordinary Animal

When aspens shiver in the dark
I understand myself.
When water tumbles over itself
under starlight, I grow in me

a second wing so I can see her:
sister, small in our father's garden
taking her time with salted snails
and desert sage. When fog-moon

rises, I want to walk back
into that walled paradise, turn into
the girl I was to tell her a story
in birdsong. I know how

to call out in the marble dawn
like a Steller's jay, afraid
of my own longing. I believe
in the river, revising,

and the mountain trickster
with its hidden penstemon, blooming
in the center of a canyon drought.
For her, I've learned to bow

without bowing. I hold thistles
in my hips for her, stand still
and strong against the ordinary
animal devouring us both.

Turn to Ash

Imagine your bird-self: white thorn and cinquefoil

winding their way

up the August mountain.

Slow moving creatures with full bones and focus

lunge through the understory.

What do they know about flower-walking, flight moons—

their clicks and their fascia, their hesitant

assembly? In the garden in childhood, you lead:

one sister pulling the other

through laughter palms, jasmine. Then two turn to ash

scattered by sons over phantom orchids.

Now the lake dawns with blue defeat—

a bottled invitation. You sing again your fear-song

certain she's somewhere in the morning light.

III

LETTER TO MY MOTHER

Song: *my beloved mother. Oh: me, survivor.*
My lyrics: forged from the awe that is my life . . .
   —Janelle Saito

I'm brought close by the spirits tonight to your voice.

My machine cycles through songs and soundtracks,

beats and melodies and lands on a recording:

us in a restaurant—seaside, 2011—talking family

and farms, two heart attacks for Grandpa, too much fish,

and the legacies of sons. Where were we?

You're here with me, though I'm two states east,

in an artist's outpost in the highland desert

divinating history. Today I found a photo

in Densho's Gila River archives of a man—a farmer?—

keeping watch over new blooms in a flower nursery,

where "much experimentation is being done to develop

strains of flowers which will thrive in hot, dry climate."

I think of your father, farmer of grapes in that tiny town

outside of Fresno, striving to bring the land to life,

tying the vines, pruning, spraying, digging water trenches

with a crew—sometimes—but often alone. You survived him.

You and your two brothers—three chased and chasing

tumbleweeds—making your way while your mother worked

and fog unlaced the winter orchards. What goes underground

when the earth shakes? When the farm fails and the father,

lost at the bar, goes absent; what went quiet in you?

Some rivers aren't visible to us; their waters rush beneath soil.

Some spaces exist between letters and words,

awaiting ignition. I think of our rage. I think of Leigh's

tenderness and the lungs of grief, joy anthems, the dead's

desire, the saguaro storing all that water and bloating

because of it. I think of the illusion of silence, the illusion of stillness, and this spinning rock, spinning within and beyond

our bodies. Now I understand: You came across twice to us

in different forms: Eight-armed protector and strumming, humming

songstress; flame and holly field; the goddess of water

and the Korean Shaman, healing our vision by blinding

the third eye—that power and mercy, laced like snakes in you.

"She was now the center of what surrounded her,"

writes John Berger. "All that was not her made a space for her."

All that was not her made a space for her. You return me

to the axial age and the dignity of consequences, mother.

You re-mother. *Song* is your name, and the *oh* of awe,

and the promise of time-space expanding.

—*June 20, 2019. Santa Fe, NM.*

Three Sijo

for M, M, and J

Photos make   rage flat: your life
       traded for   soy, sacks of rice.

Hair dust-white   cool folded face
       beneath two flags   beneath husband.

What props up   heaven in you?
       Four daughters   two sons.

Nights alone   and staring, sure
       of ocean traffic   and thin smoke

uncoiling   cresting up from
       Broadway below.   Small-waisted

grandmother   city girl in '46.
       I see you fighting in   two languages.

Mother, I watch.   Strong, you walk tall
        reflecting mountains.   Water grows

more sure of   its strength as rain
        rushes beneath   cool elm winds.

You are not   anymore a shard.
        History's strong song   carves us whole.

How to Prepare the Mind for Lightning

In the recesses of the woman's mind
    there's a warehouse. The warehouse
        is covered in wisteria. The wisteria wonders

what it's doing in the mind of the woman.
    The woman wonders too.
        The river is raw tonight. The river is a calling

aching with want. The woman walks towards it
    her arms unimpaired and coated
        with moonlight. The wisteria wants the river.

It also wants the warehouse in the mind
    of the woman, wants to remain in the ruins
        though water is another kind of original ruin

determined in its structure and unpredictable.
    The woman unlaces the light across her body.
        She wades through the river while twining wisteria

bleeds from her mouth, her eyes, her wrist-veins,
    her heart valve, her heart. The garden again
        overgrows the body—called by the water

and carried by the woman to the wanting river.
    When she bleeds the wisteria, the warehouse
        in her mind is free and empty and the source

of all emptiness. It's free to house the night sky.
It's free like the woman to hold nothing
but the boundless, empty, unimaginable dark.

LINES FOR A FUTURE CHILD

with lines from Mitsuye Yamada's Desert Run

A certain quiet tonight, a certain sanctuary. I cultivate a
nostalgia for the present.

Moonrise over mesquite and me in the outer-dark away
from the orbits, dreaming your face.

My desert never ages

If you must fit me to your needs / I will die / and so will you

So I dream a life beyond mine with dark matter desire. I
study the creosote's tears.

Feel worlds inside of this one, laboring into birth.

Feel garden caves beneath the soil where dead dance and
roots lock arms, drinking water.

Their roots spread / wide on the surface / expecting / drops
/ of my blood

In New York and young, I worried about sunlight. I
stood in the broken theater beside my sisters, stage
bashed and bleeding with red signs of hate.

I am back to claim my body

I was too young to hear silence before

Now I stroke a small lump in the mysterious slope
between thigh and lower belly and terror sings through
me like a corrugated flame.

I return to the desert

Everything is done in silence here

In the world I imagine for you, women of the deep rise
from the red rocks, hauling from the bogs our prehistory.

The canyon is a place with eyes.

The desert is the lungs of the world

As a ghost, I grow stronger and lighter at the same time.

I am transfused / by the creosote / shrubs

I talk stories to your daughters' daughters from the
desert ruins.

Days I Can't Feel You

after Alexis Pauline Gumbs

I dive my body into the deep end, pluck golden leaves
    from the silty bottom, nearly drown.

I push my body against concrete, surrender
    to ribboning light, grow rapturous

in the gravity of quiet. Days I can't see you
    I continue my study of beaked whales

and pink dolphins—mystery species
    who survive by going stealth, unsurveilled

by the terror. Away from the carnival
    of recognition, I could be the moon.

I could mother myself by swimming circles
    around an absence until it speaks.

Whatever in me might nourish you
    mends itself in the undrowned part of the planet

that navigates by the depths of untraceable tongues.
    Days I can't feel you I let myself feel you.

I study the blueprints of bioluminescence
    in underwater caves. You do not dim.

LETTER TO MY SISTER

In a dream, I found her skull in a closet. It started to speak.
—Leigh Saito

Do you ever feel alive with someone else's memories?

Here in the mountains of Summit County,

the afternoon light strikes sudden then retreats.

Rivers disappear underground; rocks, water-worn,

carry their own emptiness. Do you remember the story

of the abandoned girl raised by cranes and sea dragons

among mountain goddesses? Or the tale

of the Buddhist woman who returns to her hometown

to meet the part of her spirit that never left, the part that grew

more and more ill until the two pieces of her soul rejoined?

Those girls in their father's garden—where did they go?

Last week, swells of bodies flooded streets with fists

and human sounds—breathtaking grief, generative rage.

I'm starting to believe in frontline beyond our skin,

our bodies no longer turning against our bodies,

our recovery occurring through regeneration:

the uncommon animal, newborn and strong, galloping

through the third space and activating

with her motion the desirable world. In the highest town

in North America, mine pilings mount memories

of their old defense; roofs kneel to the barren sky;

mountain shadows, ancient and electric, sweep the lower valleys.

I wish I could box these vistas and sunlight flickering

through eye-knotted aspens, send them westward

to your coastal city, a metropolis under siege. Do you ever

feel alive with someone else's memories, ancestral animals

incepted in nightmares, projected in dreams? I miss you

like I miss my life. I live alongside our past now—

the only doorway to the future.

—June 16, 2020. Frisco, CO.

SELF DISGUISED AS MY FATHER'S GARDEN

1.

Goddess of dormancy   Goddess of unsilent
silence: Return me to the tangle

of rosemary   in the company of foxes
and midnight fish ghosts in the half-built pond

I'm a layer of ash along Father's maple   Porous netleaf
frosted jasmine prostrate to secret rains

Was it ever a question of propagation?
Autotrophic witness to daughterhood

to acacia bloom and dove song   I no longer
turn against myself   give knee and tongue

and nipple and eyelash   to grass beneath Mother's palm
to fist-sized stones gathered by Father

from riparian meadows   Soil: conspire
I'm several joys ahead now   Eremitic bone story

a parliament of orange blossoms
falling on Stone Buddha

2.

Against waterless ideologues

        Against ordinary animals   with extraordinary train of ghosts

    Against dominion   of white space

        and industrial valleys   Against childhood Polaroid

with unshut eyes   Against bullets in blue fog   boys in the bar

    Against shot lessons and poker smoke   soaking the motherline

        yellowing ceiling   Against chemical sleep

in designated light   Against uprooted myrtle

        and Earth store   Against war

3.

You along the pebbled path   in a former century asking your father
        the names of trees   making up

for nothing.   *Camphorwood, Agapanthus, Asian Pear.*   Dauntless
        winter sun over the fog lake   torches the backyard's eleventh hour.

You speak the names slowly   *Compact Nandina, Blue Bird Jade*   earth tides
        drawing you closer to sky.   Early palace gardens

harvested emptiness   white gravel courtyards   containing nothing,
        awaiting the kami's arrival.   From where I belong

to the ancient future   I hear you forging a wail-less birth:
        midlife valley solstice   another failed year   the Japanese Black Pine

and other strappy evergreens   lending their shadow to your late-stage rapture.
        Magnolia, Azalea, Coral Bark Maple.   Childless elder daughter

have you said the hardest thing?   Your father's corded brow   is one site
        of eternity.   His silence is the shape   of a crane's back

an emptiness so full   you had no choice but perennial arrival.
        Plum Yew, Bloodgood, Cypress, Stone.   Despite your whispered armature

I hear your beveled plea   its shaded desires   your rhizomatic
    runaway love throttling through the infrared   landscape of zeros.

Your heart sounds in surrounding air.   The call of his name
    is stronger than barbed wire.

Dear Damselfly

All summer long, the red-fur rhubarb crosses over.

Spirits fight up through the scallions
wasps shadow the crocuses
with their family talk.

I travel from June to June
seeking a beauty like yours:
kiss-shaped, unstandardized
coptering the long grass
like a news flight over Manhattan.

What have I loved? The tended soil
and the thrashing that breaks it.

Gray-skinned stems, dying and alive
cycle up the lattice. Bees drone the sound-wound
the sunny hum of community.

You with your smoke-eyes are all-seeing
predaceous and singular over lake waters.

De-root me from this garden.

Lines for a Future Essay

with lines from Kim Hyesoon, Valarie Kaur, Brandon Shimoda,
John Holloway, Jaime Rodríguez-Matos, Reginald Shepherd

If I had the right metaphor for these tumors, benign and growing—a
commensurate language—

One story I tell myself: each masking smile and night-clench of teeth,
each voiceless committee meeting and waiting out the mountain wasps,
each stifled cry and man stumbling drunk to touch me, each unforgiv-
ing asphalt sky—

Made a mark in me.

Do you hear the voice of the inside? The child's unconscious floating the
shadowed ridge?

What does it feel like in your body?

Death is alive with answers.

It's true I've wanted a child.

What did I expect? One anviling heart making a home in my rib cage?
It wasn't like that. It was us in the highland desert, light as cirrus
clouds and divining new mythologies with incense smoke.

In the throes of the pandemic, I agreed to get married to a brighter him.

In the horizon dream, my grandparents are finally—in the year 2020—
returning from the desert camp. They drop their suitcases on my
current porch and enter happily, no terror in their seams.

In my home, I make a bed for them.

The ancestors are always arranging, the hands reaching from all generations to locate me in a body that is also theirs.

The performer cannot develop her body and soul, her life as the performer of the Abandoned, without making contact with ghosts.

Hannah says it's common in Korea: women, their hysterectomies. My mother and her mother and my sister and me, doubled over in a similar ocean.

Sometimes the cysts are submerged stalactites. Aperture of wildflowers, emergent in the womb, seeding my uterus. Heart-shaped flames in the tumescent dark.

We think we are society. We are not nouns. We overflow.

Will I give birth to fire? Will I give birth to stones?

I went into my home by planetary force.

I went into my home and made a bed for them.

It's true I've wanted a child.

Someone comes from another dimension and touches you. The absence is as important as the feeling of presence.

New life in the riverstream of ancestors, that's what it felt like: history obliterating history for the wholeness of the stone.

That's what it felt like: romance coating a city of sage, *the poet created by the poem.*

Muscle branch of memory: bone-tender, mesquite-strong. One soul then another soul piercing the din, rising in resistance.

How or what did you feel when you visited Poston and Gila River?

In the highland desert, he took my hand—

Ars Poetica

Exit the nameless sickness in the spiral process—

this writing, that is,

this performance with ghosts.

Exit this season of yellow jackets and spruce-veins—

underground colonies

and temple-less temples

in the formless sea.

Surrender to the modern light—

perpetual horizon, muddy emergence, fertile abyss.

I'm rehearsing my arrival now—

recovering madness by light of the moon-fist—

herstory and herstory and herstory

fracturing the space of the real.

Letter to Brandon

It is too soon and too late, though mostly too late, and on time . . .
—Brandon Shimoda

Yesterday, blackbirds rose from the high brush

near the stone memorial at Poston while my dad

flung his arms out, marveling and smiling in the sweet

unseasonal winds. A half-moon hung above

the circle of palm trees in the morning light.

Weathered folded cranes lay slumped at the base

of the memory marker. Is it too soon to be writing this?

Is it too late? You once told me about prisoners

in the Department of Justice camp at Fort Missoula

collecting stones and speculating on the ancient rivers

and seas that made them. Driving with my father

from California through Joshua Tree and on to Arizona

I felt the smallness of the human project

against primordial ridge lines and desert seafloor.

I felt the seabed and the wild sea.

Now I hear him coughing in the next room

in a stranger's house in the warm hour of Phoenix,

having visited two prison camps this week

and communed. Having driven together

in my tiny Honda up rock-strewn acres

to the bright stone monument with our two guides

from the Gila River Indian Community.

Under the high, white afternoon, over the olive trees

and mesquite, I felt the bodies of our elders

blooming in the steady heat—rising up, rising and rising.

Brandon, maybe we are who we remember ourselves

to be. Our precarious lives, an act of resistance.

Our survival, a rebellion. "Our ancestors were here together," said our guides, "Stolen bodies on stolen lands."

So the four of us stood in a circle and the wind stood

with us and memories made us stronger: tractor rides

and bartered pomegranates; koi ponds, talent shows,

night shootings, urns. Dear Brandon, Nikiko,

Mia, Todd; Dear Brian, Patricia, Koji, Sean—

Didn't we dance? Didn't we rise from July's belly

—Bon Odori—moving to Taiko stomps

in the circle of families, learning the shapes of honor

early on? We were site-specific and dangerous

in our pleasure. We were talk-story breathless laughter

and ancestral rage. Now I hear violins singing

in the barrack bones, eighty years on. Creosote overtakes

the old foundations, its healing spines break concrete.

"Is it possible to send promises backwards?"

Tell me, Brandon, what do you think?

—*May 27, 2019. Phoenix, AZ.*

Last Lines (II)

Toothless starlight, sing to me now.

Low moon, skin-swaddled and ancient, speak from the eye of the
atmosphere—loosely livid, dropped under.

Carved smoke, red water, neck ache—

Whatever ate their hearts has spared you; start living in reverse.

You are allowed to begin somewhere.

You are allowed to change.

And why *not* the body? Nipple and hip crease, mountain fibroma,
desmoid tumor dance and two hands clasping, unclasping.

Water molecules under anger shape-shift, the past is like that.

A single crane rises from a watery roadside ditch like a letter.

Gnostic in the oak-light, bring me to my senses in the tired dawn.

Pack of dogs, take my palm.

Now you get to believe in God, all of the blessings so unclear.

Now starlings sing verses, cloud-light swells the grape fields.

How long before you give yourself to moonlight fanatical?

How long before you recall the taste of democracy, rock-shore to sea's rain, the people's eternal return?

Yellow cedar, un-shard me.

Beautiful prayer animal, rise to the occasion of your living.

NOTES

"Letter to My Father." The letter correspondences began after my dad and I visited the ruins of the Gila River prison camp located on the sovereign land of the Gila River Indian Community (GRIC) in Arizona. It was there that his parents, Alma and Mitsuo Saito, were incarcerated during World War II, along with over 13,000 people of Japanese ancestry. We also visited the Poston monument, a memorial for the prison camp located on the Colorado River Indian Tribes' land. We are grateful to Mr. Cody Cerna and Mr. Wally Jones, members of the GRIC, who accompanied us on our visit. To read the complete letter exchanges with Brandon Shimoda, Nikiko Masumoto, my mother, father, sister, and community friends including Marion Masada, Saburo Masada, Valarie Kaur, Devoya Mayo, Akiko Miyake-Stoner, Naser Nekumanesh, Tess Taylor, Lee Herrick, Lisa Lee Herrick, Nohemi Samudio Gamis, Samina Najmi, and Amy Uyematsu visit https://www.youaremissing.com/

"February 19, 1942." The title marks the date that Executive Order 9066 was signed by President Roosevelt, initiating the mass forced removal and incarceration of Japanese immigrants and Japanese American citizens living on the West Coast. To learn more about the WWII-era incarceration of the Japanese American community, visit www.densho.org.

"Thirteen Ways of Looking at a Teacher Resource." The questions in this poem are from educational material associated with a group exhibition entitled "From Generation to Generation: Inherited Memory and Contemporary Art," installed at the Contemporary Jewish Museum in San Francisco in 2016. "Even the dead will not be safe from the enemy if he wins" is from Walter Benjamin's 1940 essay, "Theses on the Philosophy of History."

"Theses on the Philosophy of History." "Capitalism walks on water" is a reference to Tongo Eisen-Martin's poem, "It's Midnight Already."

"Self-Portrait Disguised as Memory Hunter." "Feel America / Live America / Love America / Then work" is from Georgia O'Keeffe's writings, housed at the Georgia O'Keeffe museum in Santa Fe, New Mexico.

"Letter to My Grandmother." "Empathy is a smooth stone that cuts sometimes" is quoted from Sara Konrath. The subsequent metaphors were cowritten with Traci Brimhall.

"Lines for a Future Essay." ". . . the voice of the inside" and "The performer cannot develop her body and soul, her life as the performer of the Abandoned, without making contact with ghosts" are from Kim Hyesoon's *Princess Abandoned*. Thank you to Mariah Bosch for sharing this text with me. "The ancestors are always arranging, the hands reaching from all generations to locate me in a body that is also theirs" is from Brandon Shimoda's *The Grave on the Wall*. "We think we are society. We are not nouns. We overflow" is pieced together from John Holloway's *In, Against, and Beyond Capitalism: The San Francisco Lectures*. "Someone comes from another dimension and touches you. The absence is as important as the feeling of presence" is from a personal correspondence with Jaime Rodríguez-Matos. "the poet created by the poem" was inspired by Reginal Shepherd's writing on Octavio Paz: "Octavio Paz has pointed out that the poet is only a poet because of the poem: it creates him as much as he creates it," from Shepherd's *Orpheus in the Bronx: Essays on Identity, Politics, and the Freedom of Poetry*. "How or what did you feel when you visited Poston and Gila River?" is from a personal correspondence with Brandon Shimoda. "What did it feel like in your body?" is from a personal correspondence with Valarie Kaur.

Well Brynn—I could only say, the trip we did together was eye opening and very heart warming. What made me feel that way was that you were there and my own parents were there at one time. I guess I felt a presence of something living and something that has passed. To be in a place that I couldn't imagine how people felt and lived.

You know I love to garden, move rocks, shovel dirt and grow vegetables. But to see what they did in the camp with the landscape was amazing. This place was dry and barren. From afar, it looks dry and barren. But to me it was an unbelievable sight. The foundations, the manzanita plants, the broken glass and the amazing koi ponds. How did they do this?

What's ironic Brynn—my parents wanted to forget this place—but I want to remember it.

Thanks for the memory. Always, Your Dad